SPIDERS SET I

JUMPING SPIDERS

Tamara L. Britton
ABDO Publishing Company

visit us at
www.abdopublishing.com

Published by ABDO Publishing Company, 8000 West 78th Street, Edina, Minnesota
55439. Copyright © 2011 by Abdo Consulting Group, Inc. International copyrights
reserved in all countries. No part of this book may be reproduced in any form without
written permission from the publisher. The Checkerboard Library™ is a trademark and
logo of ABDO Publishing Company.

Printed in the United States of America, North Mankato, Minnesota.
042010
092010

 PRINTED ON RECYCLED PAPER

Cover Photo: Peter Arnold
Interior Photos: Alamy pp. 10, 12, 17, 19; Corbis p. 5; Getty Images pp. 6–7, 11, 15;
    iStockphoto pp. 9, 18; Peter Arnold p. 16; Photo Researchers p. 21

Editor: Megan M. Gunderson
Art Direction & Cover Design: Neil Klinepier

Library of Congress Cataloging-in-Publication Data

Britton, Tamara L., 1963-
  Jumping spiders / Tamara L. Britton.
      p. cm. -- (Spiders)
  Includes index.
  ISBN 978-1-61613-441-9
  1. Jumping spiders--Juvenile literature. I. Title.
  QL458.42.S24B75 2011
  595.4'4--dc22
                          2010013425

Of all the spider families, the jumping spider's is the largest!

Sizes

Jumping spiders are small to medium sized. The average body size is 0.4 to 1 inch (1 to 2.5 cm) long. Yet with thousands of species in their family, jumping spiders come in many sizes!

One of the largest North American jumping spiders is the regal jumping spider. It lives in the southeastern United States. Females are 0.3 to 0.9 inches (0.7 to 2.2 cm) long. Males are smaller. They reach just 0.2 to 0.7 inches (0.6 to 1.8 cm) in length.

The tiny male dimorphic jumping spider has brightly colored pedipalps. He uses them to catch a female's attention during mating season!

The daring jumping spider is found east of the Rocky Mountains. This large jumping spider grows from 0.3 to 0.8 inches (0.7 to 1.9 cm) in length. Females are slightly larger than males.

SHAPES

With so many species, jumping spiders also have a variety of body shapes. Most jumping spiders have hairy, heavy bodies. A few are very slender. Some even look like ants!

The jumping spider's two body sections are the **cephalothorax** and the **abdomen**. The cephalothorax is the front body part. It contains the spider's brain, **venom** glands, and stomach.

Six pairs of **appendages** attach to the cephalothorax. At the spider's head are two **pedipalps**. Between them are two **chelicerae**. The chelicerae are tipped with fangs!

Next, four pairs of short, strong legs line the sides of the cephalothorax. Claws at the end of each leg help the spider grip onto surfaces.

Spider Anatomy

SPINNERETS

ABDOMEN

CEPHALOTHORAX

PEDICEL

PEDIPALP

CHELICERA

LEG

The jumping spider's intestine, nerve cord, and blood vessels pass through the pedicel. This slim waist connects the **cephalothorax** with the **abdomen**.

The abdomen contains the jumping spider's heart. It also holds its **digestive** tract, reproductive and respiratory **organs**, and silk glands. The silk glands make the spider's silk. The spider releases the silk from its body through its spinnerets.

COLORS

Most jumping spiders are not very colorful. They are usually a dark color with lighter markings. But some species are brightly colored. Their bodies may have fancy patterns and designs.

Daring jumping spiders are black or brown. There are white spots on their **abdomens** and legs. These otherwise drab spiders have bright green **chelicerae**!

One of the most boldly colored jumping spiders is the magnolia jumping spider. Its bright green body is

The magnolia jumping spider can move each eye independently!

The daring jumping spider is also called the bold jumping spider.

perfect for the spider's leafy **habitat**. Like most spiders, this camouflage hides the magnolia jumping spider from predators.

WHERE THEY LIVE

Jumping spiders live all over the world. They can be found on every continent except Antarctica. They are most abundant in warm, tropical locations.

Wherever they live, jumping spiders like to be in the sun. They seek

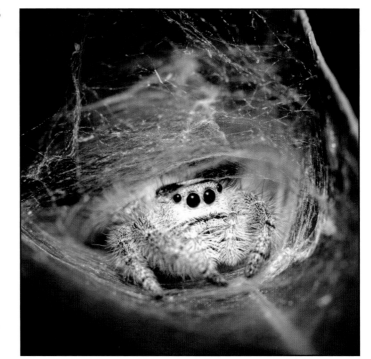

A jumping spider's nest

Where Do Jumping Spiders Live?

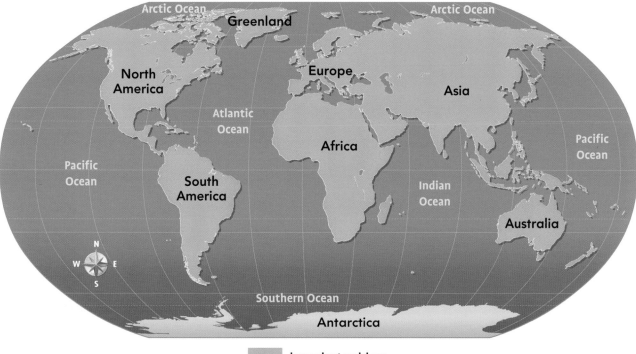

jumping spiders

out sunny dwellings in woodlands, **pastures**, and **heaths**. Jumping spiders live by themselves, though sometimes a male will nest near a female.

Jumping spiders nest in bark, stones, and leaves. They don't spin webs to live in. Instead, they use silk from their spinnerets to line their nests. This creates a tightly woven silk padding.

SENSES

Of all the world's spiders, jumping spiders have the best vision. They can recognize shapes. And, they can spot prey up to 12 inches (31 cm) away!

Jumping spiders are often recognized by the arrangement of their eyes. Their eight eyes are in four rows that make a W-shaped pattern.

Two small eyes form the top row. The next row has two very tiny eyes. These four eyes sense movement.

The third row consists of two medium-sized eyes. These eyes determine distance. These eyes sit just outside the two largest eyes, which make up the bottom row. With these eyes, the spider sees focused, color images.

Jumping spiders can also taste and smell. They do this with hollow hairs at the ends of their **pedipalps** and legs.

Jumping spiders have well-developed eyes. They see images in sharp detail and full color.

DEFENSE

Some jumping spiders resemble ants. Predators who dislike ants leave these sneaky spiders alone!

Many predators like to eat jumping spiders. The spiders use camouflage to defend themselves. Even brightly colored species are difficult to see in their **habitats**. For example, the regal jumping spider easily blends in with tree bark.

What if jumping spiders can't fool their predators with camouflage? Then they may rear back into a threat position. Luckily, jumping spider **venom** is

Camouflage allows a spider to hide in plain sight!

not poisonous to humans. But if they have to, they will bite!

If all else fails, the jumping spider can simply jump away. Some species can jump as far as 40 times their own body length!

FOOD

Jumping spiders are hunting spiders. They do not catch their food in a web. Instead, these carnivores actively seek out insects and other spiders.

A jumping spider hunts during the day. It hunts like a cat does. First, the spider uses its excellent

Jumping spiders help control insect pests.

vision to locate its prey. Then, the spider slowly stalks its victim. When the spider gets close enough, it uses its strong legs to pounce on the prey!

As the spider jumps, it releases a silk line from its spinnerets. This lifeline keeps the spider from falling. If the spider misses its prey, it can use the line to climb back to where it started. Then, the hunt begins again!

After a successful hunt, the spider **injects** its prey with **venom**. Then, it spits **digestive** juices on its victim. This liquefies the prey's **tissues**. The spider then sucks up its liquid meal.

BABIES

When he is ready to mate, a male jumping spider must attract a female. To do this, he waves his **pedipalps** in a special way. Using her excellent vision, the female recognizes the male. She then allows him to approach her.

After mating, a female jumping spider spins a silken pad. She lays more than 100 eggs on the pad. Then, she wraps the pad in more silk to form an egg sac.

The baby spiders are called spiderlings. When they hatch, the spiderlings spin some silk. The wind catches the silk and carries them through the air. This is called ballooning. Some spiderlings land on a nearby plant or rock. Others rise thousands of feet in the air and land far away!

The female jumping spider guards her eggs until they hatch.

After landing, the spiderlings look for nesting sites. As they grow, they will **shed** their **exoskeleton**. This is called molting. Soon, the spiders are mature and seek out mates of their own. Male jumping spiders do not live long after mating. Females live for about two years.

GLOSSARY

abdomen - the rear body section of an arthropod, such as an insect or a spider.

appendage - a smaller body part that extends from the main body of a plant or an animal.

cephalothorax (seh-fuh-luh-THAWR-aks) - the front body section of an arachnid that includes the head and the thorax.

chelicera (kih-LIH-suh-ruh) - either of the front, leglike organs of an arachnid that has a fang attached to it.

digestive - of or relating to the breakdown of food into simpler substances the body can absorb.

exoskeleton - the outer covering or structure that protects an animal, such as an insect.

habitat - a place where a living thing is naturally found.

heath - open, barren land with low-growing bushes.

inject - to force a fluid into the body, usually with a needle or something sharp.

organ - a part of an animal or a plant composed of several kinds of tissues. An organ performs a specific function. The heart, liver, gallbladder, and intestines are organs of an animal.

pasture - land used for grazing.

pedipalp (PEH-duh-palp) - either of the leglike organs of a spider that are used to sense motion and catch prey.

Salticidae (sahl-TIHSUH-dee) - the scientific name for the jumping spider family.

shed - to cast off hair, feathers, skin, or other coverings or parts by a natural process.

tissue - a group or cluster of similar cells that work together, such as a muscle.

venom - a poison produced by some animals and insects. It usually enters a victim through a bite or a sting.

WEB SITES

To learn more about jumping spiders, visit ABDO Publishing Company on the World Wide Web at **www.abdopublishing.com**. Web sites about jumping spiders are featured on our Book Links page. These links are routinely monitored and updated to provide the most current information available.

INDEX